Where Did Summer Go?

Poetry By

Joel Williams

Joel Williams

Published By

Vabella Publishing

PO Box 1052

Carrollton, Georgia 30112

Copywrite © 2023 by Joel Williams

All rights reserved. No part of this publication may be produced, stored in a retrieval system, or transmitted in any form by any means such as: electronic, mechanical, photocopying, recording, or otherwise, without prior permission from the author.

ISBN: 979-8-89450-010-2

Printed In The United States Of America

Joel Williams

For Jeannie

Acknowledgements

Many thanks to the *prodder extraordinaire*, Beverly Bruemmer for prodding. I need that old kick in the rear to get anything done. She can prod in the nicest way. Equally adept at what she does is our editor Amber Pickle. Amber can magically do away with all my mistakes in grammar and style. Thank you, Amber . And thank you, John Bell, for being a publisher that accepts the author who has no idea what they are doing.

I must also acknowledge, as usual, my wife Jeannie for her patience and encouragement through this entire process. Our children, grandchildren,— and now, great grandchild, Camryn Anne, are constant inspirations for the poems in this publication.

To you, the reader, thanks for your time and indulgence in my attempts to put in writing what I enjoy expressing.

And to God for these words.

God And The Wasp

He flew away when I sat down.
I was glad he was gone.
He's such a small creature
against my bulk and brawn.

Previous encounters, however,
had taught me to respect
the fact that brawn and bulk
cower to this insect.

To my dismay, he returned
and alighted on my hand.
I dared not twitch a muscle
lest he misunderstand.

As he explored my fingers
I prepared for the sting.
I queried "Should I knock him off?"
or pray he'll soon take wing.

So I opted to bring God into the fray
and quiz Him of this creature.
I wondered if He knew it's purpose
when He designed its every feature.

For it looks to be a composite
of three distinct sections—
head, body, and stinger
with little apparent connections.

But I'm sure that God had fun
when He laid out this design
Add antenna, legs and wings
and connect all with a spine.

Could ever a human mind create such a marvel
and give it purpose in creation?
Could a human create a new creature
and claim innocence from imitation?

What features of design would one use
that God has not previously framed?
If challenged to create something no one ever has,
is there a graphic image that remains unnamed?

For every pen mark on the designer's pad
bespeaks the great creator's hand,
and the wasp was designed to perfection
And God said, "It's good, just as I planned."

Joel Williams

Ode To A Beautiful Woman
For Jeannie

When rhyme's muse invades the heart
and words of beauty sought
to write an ode to the fairest woman
that ever heaven wrought,
then familiar words pale as they creep
into the abyss,
and sputter to a darkened grave
that the poet must dismiss.
For words that describe such beauty
have yet to be spoken;
words like "pretty, fair, or lovely"
are but a paltry token.

So the poet weds poetry with its sisterly Muse
and tones and words unite to form new virtues
that make verbal discourse and audible
sound a paean
to the indescribable beauty of the female being.

Where Did Summer Go?

Could ever a musician pluck the lyre
and play a song so sweet
that its tones evoke that moment where
past and future meet?
If yea, this musician must study the technique
of the lyre,
and find the purest tones to which
musicians aspire.
For these tones bespeak the quietude
to which her solitary thoughts allude.

But then, the aulos may be lustily sounded
to describe where her raucous
side is founded.
Bacchus would welcome her
devilish delight
as she dances with moonbeams
in fanciful flight.
She loved to be near the ocean
in the days of her youth.
Questioned of her love, she alone knows
the truth.

Joel Williams

She often dons the garments that let her
softness speak;
Then swiftly changes to the
cloak of mystique.
She dresses for a party where
she's queen of the ball
and stirs the hearts of many
as she glides through the hall.

Her face is defined by the classic silhouette
and kept in Eros' quiver as a treasured secret,
to be released as an arrow, a onetime dart
that will fly straight and true
to a lover's heart.
Her features are classic and
modern entwined,
the portrait every artist begs to find.

Her lineage might well include
Psyche or Aphrodite;
Goddesses whose beauty enticed the mighty,
and threatened their kingdoms
with ruin and decline;
more intoxicating than the finest red wine.
Beauty, personified in womankind,
is God's gift enshrined.

Where Did Summer Go?

Joel Williams

Freedom's High

The bird does not belong in a cage.
She was given wings to fly.
Tho' the cage be gilded gold,
freedom's fancy is in her eye.

If the cage door be loosened,
she seeks the open sky.
Never to the cage will she return
upon feeling freedom's high.

HOMELESS

The man in the tent beside me is
high on cocaine.
He's tried to shake the habit, but the drug has
staked its claim.
He's a shell of a man who makes his living;
begging on the corner for whatever one is giving.

He once stood proud in defense
of his nation;
now he's consumed with
guilt and humiliation.
Cars pass without stopping, people look
the other way.
"You're just a bum. Get a job," they say.

He wakes during the night;
I hear him scream.
We all share some version of that
recurring dream:
Blood, guts, that smell, those screams,
body parts flying,
bombs, rockets, grenades,
and bold men crying.

These are the pictures that torture the mind.
Those who survived grieve those left behind—
their buddies who died in their arms;
their friends.
They see the fear that froze their eyes
as life ends.

Three tents down, is Lucy,
who served as a nurse.
She is a quiet one, but her eyes belie a curse.
Her eyes have witnessed more horrors
than most have ever seen.
She leaves our village at dusk
in her camouflage green.

She's a regular in the bars;
the men treat her well.
She awakes in the morning and
slips from the motel.
She comes back to the village and
bathes in the stream.
She scrubs relentlessly to cleanse
herself of shame.

Where Did Summer Go?

Eighteen years on the marble marker;
that's his life on earth.
For the record, here's what his life was worth;
no children, no wife, no bank account, no home.
Who remembers him now that his life is gone?

Hal was probably joking with his driver
as they hit the IED;
He was a happy kid, his spirit roamed free.
Now his plot of ground is desolate,
the grass grows tall.
No one seems to remember
he gave his all.

Joel Williams

They call us *the homeless*,
the forgotten few.
Normalcy is a fleeting word on which
psychologists chew.
Some of us live in the woods,
some in the city streets.
some sleep in cardboard boxes,
some on the cold concrete.

Our training gave us skills; we were
groomed to survive.
Our skills worked for some of us
but luck kept us alive.
We're a motley crew of misfits,
but we watch out for each other.
In our minds we see ourselves
as sisters and as brothers.

Agent Orange has sealed my future;
I am dying young.
Life seeks the spring
from which it has sprung.
I see another tent is gone, another
bell has rung.
Did death claim its latest or did someone
just move on?

All for some despot's greed or politicians
quest for power.
"Send the young to fight a battle while I sit in
my ivory tower."
"War is hell," except for those
who avoid the fight.
Who can stop this madness?
Can anyone make it right?

The homeless have no answer. They just exist
in some nether land.
They fight the devils in their heads
the best way they can.

Joel Williams

Miss You Little Girls

My mind's ear hears laughter and voices from the past,
but faint and faraway, as if behind a veil.
I strain to discern the sounds
but they are muffled and frail.

The laughter seems to echo
in the halls of my mind
and I'm snatched from the present
to another place and time.

I'm back in a world of ponytails,
doll houses, scuffed up knees.
There are fireflies in a jar,
first dates, sleep-over pleas.

I see good-night kisses, sisterly snuggles,
frogs and lizards, kittens and puppies;
tear-laced trips to the store
for replacement guppies.

Where Did Summer Go?

I am floundering in memories,
some exude unbridled joy, some burn;
and I fight the urge to stay,
but reality beckons my return.

So I leave this world
of false eyelashes and curls,
but know I'll be back tomorrow.
'Til then, I'll be missing you, little girls.

Joel Williams

Born A King

Born a King in a lowly stall,
The Son of God in a lowly stall,
the Savior of us all.

The inn had no room for a king to be born,
but a stable offered shelter
from the chill of the morn.
No royal crown adorned His head;
only swaddling clothes and a manger bed.

In wonder, they gaze on the newborn child,
the oxen and the sheep and the donkeys mild.
The cattle all murmur in sweet accord
at the sound of the child, Christ the Lord.

They listen as the child that Mary bore
in that candle lit stable
with dust on the floor,
announce with His cry to the heavens vast,
"Fulfilled are the prophecies of ages past."

Behold the birth of the King of Kings.
  Magnify the Lord of all nations.
  Listen to the angels as they sing
   their song of joyful adoration.

The shepherds round from out their fields
  proclaim His birth in solemn kneels,
and the footprints in the dust of the stable floor,
  tho' long blown away, live forever more.

TO DAWN

The mockingbird rehearses her song.
Sprites of sunshine sprinkle the dawn.
A sudden zephyr rustles the leaves;
the mother doe nurses her fawn.

The beginning of a new day affirms life,
and serves us with hope of a morrow,
when a new dawn will awake
and banish the night's sorrow.

Daybreak beckons to the poet
as a lover beseeches a sweetheart,
"Do not leave me now, beloved,
for I'll be saddened should we part."

The fleeting moment can hardly be recalled,
and once gone, is gone forever.
Who will charge my day if I miss you?
Will there be another you if time is severed?

So I will cherish these sights and sounds
and nourish the hours that come after.
I'll fill the minutes with hope and dreams,
with love, with joy, with laughter.

I'll greet the day with you, Dawn.
Together we'll savor the sunrise.
Then you'll be gone; I'll go alone
while embracing your fading sighs.

When the day is done,
and night's curtain is drawn,
I'll recall what's left behind
and pray for another dawn.

Joel Williams

Summer

I'm in the autumn of my years
There's just one thing I'd like to know
before winter tallies the arrears.
Where did summer go?

The Compassionate Angel

An angel flew to heaven carrying a grieving heart
and laid it before the heavenly throne.
"This heart belongs, God, to a grieving dad
whose two daughters are gone.

They left so unexpectedly
he had no chance to say 'goodbye.'
Every day I've helped him through,
I've seen tears in his eyes.

Lord, you are the great healer,
I beseech You, hear my plea.
Grant me the time to search heaven's throng
and find those who'll set him free.

I'll bring them to You, Lord,
and let You blend three hearts as one.
I'll take his heart back to him
and pray those tears be gone."

Then God replied, "You're a special angel.
Your compassion moves me so.
I'd love to give this heart freedom
but I really can't, you know.

I can't wipe away this hurt completely.
He'll always feel some pain;
The plan of life is written
to favor heaven's gain.

He's now seeing through different eyes
and feels the grief of others.
He'll work to relieve the pain
of heartbroken fathers and mothers,

who've known the pain of a child's loss,
and that, angel, is the heavenly plan;
the plan of life that's written
to favor heaven's gain.

Photo

I hope I'm not just a faded photo
in my grandkids' scrapbooks,
hidden away in an attic trunk
where no one ever looks.

I'd like to know I've given them
some of the joy they've given me.
They're reflections into the future,
our family's posterity.

I'd rather be remembered
as someone who gave them love,
and showed them that family blood
touches heaven above.

A photo on the coffee table
or on the family wall;
or beside their grandmother's picture
on the console in the hall.

I often look at the picture
of my great-grandmother and me,
and rue the fact that I never pursued
the course of her history.

I'd like to know more about her,
but I've waited far too long.
Everyone who ever knew her
has long ago passed on.

So start a scrapbook with photos and words,
not as a project of vanity,
but to give them a desire to revisit the past
and trace their ancestry.

The Gentle Soul

The gentle soul strives not for power,
nor lands to control;
but joys in the peace and calm
that dwell in the gentle soul.

Derelict Vessel

The derelict vessel sails the blue-green sea
with masts upright and sails unfurled.
Her course now determined by prevailing winds,
her soul abandoned; her fate imperiled.

What circumstances befell this fair ship
and left her void of cargo and crew?
Launched in homage to the fabled ship,
she bares the name 'Argo II.'

Was she, like her sister, built by the gods
who jealously destroyed the human crew?
Why are her lamps still burning?
What perils has she been through?

As she roams the sea, she emits a clue
in the creaks and groans of her boards.
Some say she sails for revenge,
others declare, "tis a vessel to avoid."

But sailors who've heard her sounds in the night
have heard those sounds before.
They know she's seeking her crew
to rest with them on the ocean floor.

For one-by-one, they succumbed
to the sirens in the mist;
for the gods had given them
songs too seductive to resist.

Now the gods desired the vessel
in their lust for all things grand,
for her beauty surpassed any ship
piloted and crewed by man.

Their envy of the bond of love
between the ship and her crew
fueled their plot to steal the craft
and claim the *Argo II*.

Joel Williams

The ship felt the nudge of sea creatures
against her sleek gray hull;
Dolphins, sharks and whales.
In her masts sat pelicans and gulls.

They shared the love that the sailors knew
for the ship that defied the odds,
and prayed the vessel
had the strength to defy the gods.

They guided the ship to the ocean
where the crew lay in wait,
for they'd never rest in peace
without their shipmate.

Now the ship and her crew
rest on the ocean floor,
and are chronicled in the annals
of the seaman's lore.

Where Did Summer Go?

Live Life

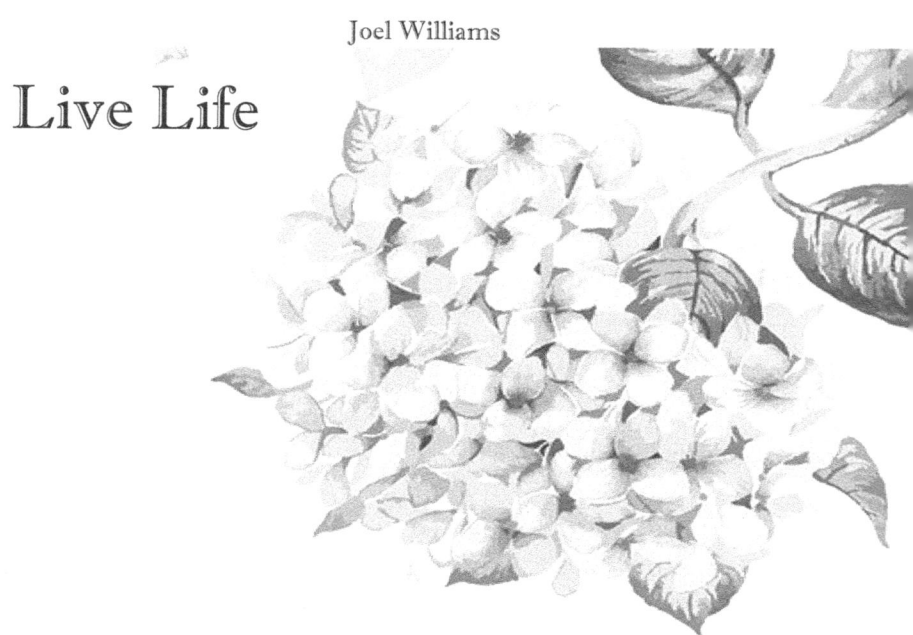

Are you still looking for a place to hang your paint-by-number art piece, or is it still in the laundry room because you think it's not good enough to hang?

If you're only waiting to fill the house with Renoirs and Monets, you'll be making a museum instead of a home. This home is you; it should reflect that. Hang that hydrangea art piece. It's beautiful and it's you.

Live life by enjoying yourself and leave some things that reflect who your were and what you were all about.

To Be A Teacher

For those who seek knowledge,
let us be a fountain.
For those who would open new doors,
let us be a key.
For those who look to higher truths,
let us be a mountain.
For those in mental bondage,
let us strive to set them free.

For the dreamer who would build a better world,
let us be the vision.
For those who yearn to fly above the crowd,
let us be wings.
For those who wish to sail beyond the horizon,
we should be a map.
For those who wish to bind nations together,
let us be the strings.

Let us teach them math, and science, and history,
art, music, literature.
Teach without prejudice, bias, or insult,
for teachers words endure.

They come to us seeking noble ideas.
Their destination to us assigned.
We believe the challenges of the future
will be solved in these young minds.

Where Did Summer Go?

Okefenokee

The glow of the moon wanes as the sun begins its reign
and the swamp sheds its nocturnal mist.
The morn reveals new beauty across the watery plain
as pine covered islands await the sun's kiss.

The swamp awakens to natures grandeur,
the sounds, the colors, the expansive scenes,
and the swamp becomes a tranquil lure,
free from the din of man's machines.

The silence is punctured by the occasional cringe
of a bull gator's roar, a hawk's shrill cry,
the soft whir of dragonfly wings,
the splash of a fish feeding nearby.

Joel Williams

The waters of the swamp are dark, opaque,
cloaking a gator to an unsuspecting prey
until the eyes in steely silence break
the surface, assessing a possible breakfast entree.

Other denizens of the swamp call it home,
making humans dichotomous strangers
to the creatures that habitually roam
the swamp, posing for invaders certain dangers.

Black bears, alligators, and venomous snakes
are camouflaged in shades of brown and gray
with yellow flies, wild boars, and bobcats that break
the night's calm with its banshee bray.

Where Did Summer Go?

A canoe's bow parts the lilies, but does so quietly,
And the paddler lifts the paddle to squelch any sound,
    for the mother gator eyes aggressors warily
should encroachment threaten her nesting mound.

Fauna and flora are delicately poised as allies,
    latching one to the other for survival.
The flesh-eating plants pose in enticing guise
    for an unsuspecting fly's arrival.

    The cypress trees spread their roots
    in the shallow waters of the lakes,
dripping moss from their cone-clad shoots,
the roots a labyrinth of hiding spots for snakes.

Joel Williams

The swamp is awash in color...
subtle... dashing... blended.
Birds, flowers, the reflections of clouds adorn the
mirror-like waters.
The great blue heron glides for a landing,
landing gear extended.
Sand hill cranes voice their concern
for they have their borders.

White Ibises, like ornaments, decorate a waterside tree.
The pileated woodpecker brandishes his red plume.
White lilies on green lily pads as far as eye can see,
like a land-locked Milky Way, on the dark waters bloom.

Botanical treasures add to the palette...
yellows... purples... pinks.
The lavender of the Swamp Iris and the Grass
Pink electrifies.
The Yellow Fringed Orchids catch the last glint
of the sun as it sinks
in the west amidst orange and pink skies.

Where Did Summer Go?

According to native inhabitants,
the land gives the swamp its name.
The word "Okefenokee" translates
to "land of the trembling earth,"
Thus, adding to the swamp's mystique
and acclaim.
This *faux land* comprises some of the
swamp's scope and breadth.

·

The settlement of peat and other materials over
thousands of years
has created a land-like stratum with water beneath.
Though weight-supporting in some areas,
the land appears
to move and tremble underneath.

Attempts to ravage the swamp's riches
have thus far been thwarted.
But a threat rises now and then
if the swamp is left unguarded.

To lose such a treasure for the sake of gain
would be a loss to the entire nation.
The Okefenokee should always remain
the pride of Georgia's population.

Pronouns

I is a pronoun. Me too.
We and they follow suit.
Some will tell you vociferously
that he and she are moot.

Many of those who would argue you down
are themselves, it seems, part of the herds
who fail to realize, in their zeal to be mod,
that pronouns are only words.

Joel Williams

Just An Angel

A whispering wind shuddered the leaves,
and dusk befell the sky.
The young lad of six or seven
wiped a tear from his eye.

For the path ahead wound through the trees
where shadows cloaked gremlins.
The boy's imagination grew intense
when he heard the leaves trembling.

His chore of retrieving the cows,
he had negligently delayed.
Now he rued his neglect
as he stood alone and afraid.

From the pasture beyond the woods
he could hear old Daisy's bell,
but between them stood the woods
where those gremlins dwell.

Where Did Summer Go?

"Maybe if I just yell," he thought,
"Maybe ol' Daisy'll hear."
Then footsteps on the path behind
froze him in fear.

A hand on his shoulder drew a fearful shriek,
and he felt another tear rolling down his cheek.

"Hi, son. I thought I'd come to help,"
said his father by his side.
The young boy grabbed his father's hand
and through tears, he replied:

"I was too scared, Dad, to go through the woods."
"I know, son," said the father. "I know.
I was watching from the barn.
I knew the sunlight had left the hollow."

As they walked together down the path
and started through the trees,
the wind chose that moment
to rustle the leaves.

"I was afraid of the sounds in the woods, Dad,"
the young boy confessed.
"Have you ever been afraid, Dad?"
The father answered, "Yes.

Everyone has felt the darkness sometime.
There's no shame to admit a fear.
The shame would be not to face it
and let it always reappear.

When I was your age and heard
frightening sounds,
your grandmother would say with a sigh,
'Just trust God to protect you, Son.
It was just an angel passing by.' "

The Best Christmas Present

You don't need paper, ribbon or bows
to wrap up the best Christmas present, you know.
You don't have to fight the crowds at the mall,
you already have the best present of all.

Just give your heart this Christmas
to the man who has no home;
to the little old woman who sits by the window
and stares at the world all alone.

Give your heart this Christmas
to the couple down on their luck
who's trying to find another nickel or dime
for a doll or a little toy truck.

Joel Williams

Give your heart this Christmas.

You'll find when you do,

you've given the best Christmas present of all

... to you ...

Mind Flurries

Mind flurries, I call them, like snow in a gusty wind.
They occur when you turn off the bed-lamp.
That's when your brain begins to spin.

Sleep is helpless against such a whirl.
Random, undisciplined thoughts take control .
Regrets of the day, concerns of the morrow unfurl.

Eleven...eleven-thirty... twelve-thirty...one
That Ambien was surely a dud.
Damn...the ticking clock just joined the fun.

The jumbled thoughts are speeding,
crashing into neighbors, pushing others aside.
Insanity appears to be breeding.

ThatmeetingtomorrowScrambleeggsFeriswheels
IshouldhavesaidtoherOfficechatterSpanishmoss
DidIrememberWhowasthatgirlPutthecatout
Usedcardeals

If I can coax sleep to take over by two,
I'll get three hours of rest.
Five a.m.'s gonna' take a serious caffeine brew.

I pray tomorrow's frets and worries
will be mild in comparison
and sleep will come easy, no mind flurries.

Birthdays

Some people love birthdays.
I'm not one of those.
A yearly reminder of mortality
is good for some, I suppose.

But the remembrance of the birthday
of a loved one gone
brings memories, then tears, then the reality
that time on earth has flown.

Then I wonder, in the stretch of my years,
when my halfway birthday came.
Was it number forty-one? Forty-two? Forty five?
And I thank God, at eighty-one, that I'm still in
the game.

Joel Williams

To Be A Dad Again

The young dad is in the park,
two children in tow.
They're riding scooters on a path
like ducklings in a row.

Mom pushes a stroller
with child number three;
They bring up the rear
of this youthful family.

After a stop for a picnic
on a table in the park,
they don their lighted helmets
for it soon will be dark.

They ride into the dusk
in the order that they came
and I thought it would be wonderful
to be that young again.

Where Did Summer Go?

How parents wish in later years
that the clock could turn around,
tick in the opposite direction,
and find their lives rewound;

to start afresh on that time-line
when their children were small
and to examine every decision they made
that could have been a better call.

To realize that time spent with a child
is more important than wealth or fame;
to realize that time with your kids is love.
When lost, it can hardly be reclaimed.

Joel Williams

Slow To Gone

The light in the eyes begins to fade ... slowly ...
slowly ...
The light never goes out; it's just edged aside by a stare.
"Who are you?" The stare asks. "Do I know you?"
The addled mind searches ... somewhere ...
somewhere.
"Maybe I'll know you tomorrow." The stare smiles.

The disease creeps in with the stealth of an incoming tide.
One enters a room and wonders why.
A memory lapse here, a forgotten name there.
"I must be getting old" becomes the alibi.
But the mind begins to close its files.

Like a discerning thief, the disease shuns the body
but slowly steals the brain.
What was an occasional slip of the mind
becomes an unrelentingly repetitive refrain.
The passageway to memory begins to clog.

The mind slowly gives in to the onslaught.
Little by little the defense is weakened, overcome.
Questions of care must be addressed.
Where will the care come from?
So many questions from a hazy fog.

While knowledge of the mind's functions
is still in the discovery stage,
the care of the victim is left to a caregiver
whose life now turns to a different page.
Different page...different book.

A caregiver's life jumps the tracks,
the derailment unexpected.
What were future plans
now seriously affected.
Life takes on a lopsided look.

One of those forks in life no one predicted,
and the path ahead is no choice at all.
The road veers left or right
and both are shrouded in a grievous pall.
The list of choices is stretched thin.

Sudden bursts of frustration become the norm
in caregiver and patient alike.
The caregiver's world, now upside down,
is like the finger in the dike.
Remove the finger and the dike caves in.

Dependence progresses, communication wanes.
The caregiver studies the seven stages
and wonders,
"What stage are we in now?
Every day a new storm, new lightnings,
new thunders."
"How long will I last?" becomes the
Caregiver's concern.

The caregiver's endurance can only survive
in the faith that God will provide a cure
before the patient fades beyond hope;
beyond the caregiver's will to endure,
beyond slow to gone and there's no return.

Joel Williams

Twilight

When twilight steals the horizon
and day is nearly done,
can I close my eyes and wonder,
"Have I done what I could have done?"

Did I ease someone's burden;
give them hope for another day?
Did I point someone to God
or did I lead someone astray?

Herein bides the tide of life
as it crashes on the shore;
"Have I done all I can?
Could I have done more?"

I didn't always listen
when I was told what to do.
I sometimes "tilted windmills"
as the winds of trouble blew.

Where Did Summer Go?

Now the twilight shadows beckon me
to recall where I've been.
Can I rid myself of guilt
as twilight filters in?

The Son of God walks in the twilight;
He touches repentant hearts.
Thus is darkness shackled
and new light and life imparts.

I thank God for His benevolence
and holding back the night.
I thank Him for the gift of time
to experience life's twilight.

Dedication of Renovation of First Baptist Church, Perry, Florida

All praise to Thee above, for by Thy hand was given this house, a bond of love, that touches earth to heaven. Its beauty shall not fade, nor time its truth destroy., with her foundation laid on Jesus Christ, her Lord?

Ol' Mitchell

Ol' Mitchel lived up the road 'bout a
half mile away,
his head prematurely bald, his beard
prematurely gray.
His children played in the broom-swept yard,
bare feet a testament, times were hard.

Ol' Mitchell was a kindly gentleman.
He and his family
lived on two acres of land on
Grandmother's farm, rent free.
He was a tenant farmer and paid his
home-place free by
planting crops on Grandmother's land
and sharing the bounty.

We called him "Ol' Mitchel" back then;
his son and me
for we were summertime buddies, when
time was free.
He and I were like brothers then
and summer seemed to have no end.

We shot our slingshots at birds
never hitting a one.
We pretended to be cowboys,

shooting our cap-guns.
We swam and fished in the pond
down behind the barn,
and listened as Ol' Mitchell spun
a ghostly yarn.

Ol' Mitchel named his son Jacob; he
was a God loving man.
He prayed every day for Jacob to live
by God's plan.
Jacob seemed to own Ol' Mitchell's heart;
dads sometimes unknowingly set one child apart.

When her mother died, grandmother
was left alone.
Compelled by her children to sell the place,
my summers with Jacob were gone.
Grandmother came to live with us in our
small borough
where people were content to live
the status quo.
Didn't see much of Jacob as we went
to different schools.
You see, we lived in the old south where
segregation ruled.

Where Did Summer Go?

Did we think about injustice in those days gone by?
I hardly think we realized how some races cry.

Ol' Mitchell died of a broken heart.
I heard through the 'vine,
that Jacob had been murdered while serving his time.
He had been arrested demonstrating for a cause,
sentenced to prison by a bending of the laws.

While defending his position, one day in the prison yard,
no one apparently watching, not even the prison guard.
He was warned he had been judged and tried.
Found in his cell the next morning; it was ruled suicide.

I stopped by Ol' Mitchell's place a few years ago;
on a southern trip to attend a business expo.
I wanted to visit his old home place;
in my mind, I'd been haunted by Ol' Mitchell's face.

The house was empty, the porch
falling down;
kudzu climbed the chimney, a cricket's chirp
the only sound.
A tear trickled down my cheek as I recalled
the memories
and I swear I heard his voice in the soft
summer breeze.

I hear you, Ol' Mitchell, and I want
you to know,
we are working to correct things, though
the process is slow.
I remember the old times when we called
each other friend
and I pray that those memories will
never end.

Jacob is still in my mind, my brother
from times past.
You both taught me long ago to eschew
such a thing as caste.
I went by your church's cemetery to pay
my respects
and saw your headstone next to one etched
with an X.

Then I remembered, Mitchell, that you never
learned to write
and I knew that you'd made that marker
and placed it on that site;
knowing that one day you'd lie next
to your son
and find your peace and rest from the race
that you'd run.

I saw that the grave next to yours had no epitaph.
Both were in disrepair, and covered with chaff.
I'll see to that, Ol' Mitchell, when I get back,
or maybe not, for it might have more impact
as a beautiful reminder
of father and son.
I'll see you, Ol' Mitchell, you and Jacob,
when we all get home.

Little Lies

Little lies nibble at truth
until the foundation quivers,
and truth crumbles like wooden bridges
in flood swollen rivers.

A little truth and a little lie
can be easily blended.
Bending words to suit advantage
can be easily defended.

Where on the x axis
does the little lie become a big one?
Are you allowed to move x right or left
just to suit the occasion?

Consequential harm of a "little white lie"
may never be revealed.
The teller goes his merry way
while the victim goes unhealed.

Where Did Summer Go?

A lie is a lie is a lie is a lie,
and never as little as one might suppose.
So if you propose to tell a little lie,
may you be reminded of Pinocchio's nose.

Joel Williams

River People

They ply the river with their crafts,
skiffs, yachts, home-made rafts;
tugs, and steamers and paddle-wheelers
carrying cotton, tourists, blackjack dealers.

River people are a unique breed,
living life by an unwritten creed;
one that binds them heart and soul
to the valleys where rivers roll.

Bound for the sea, the river holds
a mystique that beckons the bold,
ensnares the adventurer, calls to the loner
buoyed by the persuasion that the river has no
owner.

The lure to explore the next bend,
the roofless sky, the spray in the wind,
the rising moon that plays hide-and-seek
with the wispy clouds, a sudden shriek

of some night bird searching for prey,
    the eerie mists of a newborn day.

Restless, always moving with hidden dangers,
    the river coaxes unwary strangers
    with peaceful, seductive placidity
that numbs with its guise of tranquility.

It fails to warn of under-water gambles,
    mockingly serene as it ambles
through planted fields and forest glens,
through towns, under bridges as it wends
    a meandering trail to the sea
and frees itself of banks and levee.

River as a way of life sustains the soul of those
    whose livelihood ebbs and flows
    with the vitality of the river's health.
Whether seeking solitude or wealth,
river people have a growing concern
    that rivers need to return

to the hallowed reverence once shown
them by those who never tried to own
every foot of riverbank to build that second home.

Would new laws be the solution
if lawmakers were emboldened to fight pollution?

Some Random Thoughts

I wish I had known what life was all about while I was living it.

How do spiders know the exact height of your face?

Leave something beautiful when you leave.

Good poetry should paint pictures in the mind.

Where I walk God walks beside.

Joel Williams

Is God White? Is God black? Is God brown? Is God yellow? Is God red? Is God . . .

~

I've reached the ist age: cardiologist, urologist, dentist, optometrist, podiatrist, proctologist . . .

~

Will people wear clothes in heaven? Why?

~

I'm just gonna' keep praying, Lord, 'til you get tired of me asking.

~

Where Did Summer Go?

About the Author

Dr. Joel Williams' passion has always been music. He received Auburn University's first Master of Music degree, then moved his family to Tallahassee, Florida where he received a fellowship to teach while continuing his studies. He received his doctorate in music in 1986.

Tragedy struck Dr. Williams' family with the loss of two daughters. He later turned his grief over to his creative mind and his book, Poems From the Heart, was born.

His latest book, Where Did Summer Go? filled with spiritually enlightening and deeply thought provoking poetry, has proven to be just as exceptional as his first.

After many years enjoying teaching and serving as pianist for Tabernacle Baptist church, Dr. Williams retired.

Photograph by: Jeannie Williams

Dr. Williams has proven himself to be just as talented in expressing what's in his heart through poetry as he is with music.

He resides in Carrollton, Georgia with his beautiful wife, Jeannie Hudson Williams, and enjoys family life with his stepchildren, and grandchildren.

Joel Williams

www.ingramcontent.com/pod-product-compliance
Lightning Source LLC
LaVergne TN
LVHW061530070526
838199LV00010B/446